FIVE
WISHES

ALSO BY GAY HENDRICKS

At the Speed of Life

Attracting Genuine Love

Conscious Breathing

Conscious Golf

The Conscious Heart

Conscious Living

Conscious Loving

The Corporate Mystic

Lasting Love

Learning to Love Yourself

Spirit-Centered Relationships

A Year of Living Consciously

You've Got to Read This Book (with Jack Canfield)

FIVE WISHES

How Answering One Simple Question
Can Make Your Dreams Come True

GAY HENDRICKS

FOREWORD BY
Neale Donald Walsch

 New World Library
Novato, California

New World Library
14 Pamaron Way
Novato, California 94949

Design and typography by Mary Ann Casler

Library of Congress Cataloging-in-Publication Data
Hendricks, Gay.
   Five wishes : how answering one simple question can make your dreams come true / Gay Hendricks ; foreword by Neale Donald Walsch.
      p.   cm.
ISBN 978-1-57731-598-8 (hardcover : alk. paper)
1. Success. 2. Goal (Psychology) 3. Self-actualization (Psychology) 4. Life. I. Title.
BF637.S8H39 2007
158.1—dc22   2007025513

First printing, October 2007
ISBN-10: 1-57731-598-7
ISBN-13: 978-1-57731-598-8
Printed in Canada on 100% postconsumer-waste recycled paper

g   New World Library is a proud member of the Green Press Initiative.

10   9   8   7   6   5   4   3   2

For Katie —
we dreamed and wished, and it all came true.

CONTENTS

FOREWORD

This little book offers you two big gifts: a terrific story and a new way to speed up the manifestation of your goals and dreams. As a story, it's thrilling, heartwarming, and funny. As a guide to making your dreams come true, it's got a powerful new discovery that I predict will make a great deal of difference in your life.

I first heard the *Five Wishes* story during a three-hour marathon dinner aboard a cruise ship. Gay and I were seated next to each other at a table of eight people at the annual Spiritual Cinema Festival-at-Sea. Each year hundreds of fans of inspiring movies gather for a week of cinema and fun aboard a ship. This particular festival was a special one, because we were getting to see just-completed footage of the feature film made from my *Conversations with God* books.

Although we were familiar with each other's work, Gay and I didn't know each other very well on the personal level. One thing we learned quickly, though: neither of us enjoys small talk. To entertain ourselves during dinner, we took turns telling about significant events of our lives. As he finished telling the story you'll soon read, I took his arm and asked, "Have you written a book about this?"

Fortunately, he has, and now you can enjoy the story and put its powerful tools to work in your own life. If you want to know how to make your dreams come true, and you want a beautiful story to read at the same time, this book is for you.

— Neale Donald Walsch,
author of *Conversations with God*

INTRODUCTION

The Conversation That Changed My Life

Once upon a time I received the great gift of a conversation that changed my life. It ignited a hidden power in me and revealed the path to my destiny. I then found a simple process to intensify that power every day. The power and the process made it possible for me to turn all my dreams into reality.

Now I want to give you the same gift.

I want to have that conversation with you. My intention is to give you full access to this healing power. I want to show you the process and how to use it, so you can make all your dreams come true. When I received the gift, it came with the understanding that I would use it, treasure it, and pass it on to others. Now I give it to you, with the same request: Use it to hasten the manifestation of your wishes and dreams. Then pass it on to others so they can tap the power to serve their own cherished goals.

First, though, let me tell you the story, which like many stories, began on a dark and stormy night...

It was a blustery November evening in the early eighties, and I was getting dressed for a party I did not want to attend. I wanted to stay home in front of the fireplace, with a good book in my hands and a cup of steaming tea by my side. The thought of spending the next few hours with a permanent party smile frozen on my face felt about as appealing as a trip to a tattoo parlor.

I've never been a party person — something about the scattered energy and purposeless chatter usually leaves me feeling drained. However, there was another reason I was reluctant to go to this particular party. The evening was a celebration of the engagement of an oft-married friend of mine.

My friend, who was a therapist, had fallen in love again and was embarking on his fifth matrimonial adventure.

"She is the woman of my dreams," Max had told a group of us over lunch. We were all therapists, so all of us had heard this kind of breathless declaration from our clients. The trouble was that we had all heard Max say the same thing about several other women in the past. Each one remained the woman of his dreams — right up until the first time she criticized him or disagreed with him on something. Then the dream usually devolved into a squabble over real estate. The shelf life of his dream women averaged only a year or two. It was hard for me to get worked up about celebrating a new venture, since I figured it was doomed from the start.

Then there was my own stuff. I was in the early stages of my relationship with Kathlyn. Although I was deeply attracted to her, I was already feeling the early warning signs of the relationship's demise. I could feel the old, familiar fear of commitment stirring within me, the fear that filled my mind with doubt and caused me to look for things to criticize about her.

She was relatively new in town and wanted to go to the party so she could meet people. I had agreed to take her, and I didn't want to face her reaction if I changed my mind. That was another pattern of mine: to do something I didn't want to do in order to avoid the unpleasantness of the other person's disappointment or anger. Finally I decided to put aside my resistance and fulfill my obligation. I suited up, armed myself with my party smile, and marched forth into the night, headed for a party — and a conversation — that would change my life forever.

We'd been at the party about an hour, and I was dutifully shuffling around from one guest to another. I'd just about given up trying to be convivial when I was introduced to a tall fellow named Ed. His restless fidgeting suggested that he was having about as much fun as I was. I mentioned this to him, and he endeared himself to me by saying, "I loathe parties — can't stand the small talk."

I told him I felt exactly the same way.

"But I said I'd come, so here I am," he said.

Here was a man I could relate to!

"Well," he said. "Since we're here and we don't like small talk, let's not have any."

"Done deal," I said, thinking our interaction was over. Instead, it had just begun. Ed tilted his head down and looked into my eyes. "Would you like to have some big talk or no talk at all?"

I thought this over for a moment. "I vote for big talk."

"Okay. Would you like to go first?"

I shook my head. "You go first."

Ed closed his eyes for a long moment. "Well," he said, "once upon a time I almost died."

I blinked. This definitely qualified as big talk.

I waited to find out if he was going to say more. Finally I asked, "What was that like?"

"It wasn't much fun at the time," he said. "But now I think it was the best thing that ever happened to me."

"How come?" I asked.

"Because it gave me the gift of a question — a

question that I've been living with and growing with ever since."

"What was the question?" I asked.

"Are you sure you want to hear it?" he asked. "It might change your life like it changed mine."

By now I was in a state of heightened awareness. The sounds of the party had receded into a dim, distant murmur.

"Yes," I said. "I could use a life change or two right now."

He smiled and said, "Okay. Here it is. First, imagine you're on your deathbed, tonight or fifty years from now."

I'd never considered this scenario, so it took me a moment to conjure it up. Finally I saw it in my mind's eye. "Okay," I said.

"I stand by your deathbed and look you right in the eyes and ask you, 'Was your life a complete success?'"

He paused a moment while I registered the question. I nodded for him to go on.

"You might say, 'Yes, my life has been a

complete success,' or you might say, 'No, my life has not been a complete success.'"

"Right," I said, intrigued by the direction this was taking.

"If you said, 'No, my life was not a complete success,' you would have some reasons why it wasn't. For instance, J. Paul Getty, who was once the wealthiest man in the world, said on his deathbed, 'I'd gladly give up all my millions for one experience of marital happiness.' If he'd been granted a wish, that's what he would have wished for."

I was fascinated by what Ed was saying, but I could also feel a growing sense of anxiety in my belly. What did all this have to do with me?

"If you told me on your deathbed that your life had *not* been a success, what would be the things you'd wish had happened that would have made it a success?"

My mind went *tilt*. What a question!

"Before I try to answer that, Ed, would you answer a question of mine?"

He said he would.

"Who the hell are you, anyway?"

Ed laughed. It turned out I was probably the only person at the party who didn't know who Ed Steinbrecher was. As I found out, he was a famous astrologer and spiritual teacher, the favorite astrologer of many prominent people in the entertainment world, as well as the astrologer and teacher of the woman whose engagement we were celebrating.

Whoever he was, he came into my life at precisely the right time and penetrated to the heart of an issue I needed to face: What am I really doing here on this planet? What is my life purpose? Do I have a sacred mission?

I could still feel the anxiety in my belly, but I could also feel a growing sense of relief down inside. It was as if he had given me permission to drop into a level of myself I had not been able to reach on my own.

"It's a big question," I said. "Let me think about it and get back to you."

He shook his head impatiently. "The bigger

the question, the more important it is to answer it right now. This moment is all the time you need. It's the only one we have."

I felt another wave of relief. He hadn't let me, the master wriggler, wriggle off the hook. So there on the spot, I closed my eyes and took a long, slow breath. From deep inside me, I invited the answers to his question, and suddenly there they were, as if they'd been waiting all along for me to beckon them.

"Okay," I said. "Here is the number-one thing that would make my life a total success. My wish would be for a long-term, loving relationship —"

Ed stopped me, shaking his head. "Look at it from the perspective of your deathbed. Put it in the past tense, and do it first from the perspective that your life was *not* a success."

I tried again.

✦

My life was not a total success because I never enjoyed a long and happy marriage

with a woman I adored and who adored me.
I wish I'd enjoyed a lifelong blossoming of
passion and creativity with a woman.

Ed nodded. "Good. Now, tell me why that's important to you."

Even though I'd never consciously thought about why this goal was important to me, I found it easy to tell Ed my reasons; there was something about him that made deep inquiry simple and matter-of-fact. I rattled off my reasons: First, to have this kind of relationship would accomplish something I had never seen in the world, and certainly not in my family of origin. Second, to enjoy lasting love with a woman would mean that my moment-to-moment experience would be rich and joyful. Third, I had a master's degree and a PhD in counseling psychology and had counseled thousands of people on their issues and concerns. What good, I asked Ed, was all that training and practice if I couldn't learn to experience genuine, lasting love with one other human being?

Ed nodded his understanding. "Okay, now turn the wish into a goal, and put it in the present tense, as if it's happening at this moment."

I rearranged the words in my head.

✦

My life is a total success because I'm enjoying a long and happy marriage with a woman I adore and who adores me. I'm enjoying a lifelong blossoming of passion and creativity with her.

✦

I spoke it aloud to Ed, who listened carefully.

"Is that something you really want?" he asked.

"Yes."

"And is that something you're willing to commit yourself to, body and soul?"

I immediately felt a gut-dropping sensation of fear, but in spite of the wave of terror, I said, "Yes." Remarkably, as soon as I said it, the fear disappeared completely.

I felt my whole body light up with an inner smile. I had no idea if I could accomplish this goal, but I knew I would die unsatisfied if I did not commit myself body and soul to the quest. Getting clear on this goal and its importance to me awakened a burst of energy and aliveness I could feel all over.

"Okay," Ed said. "Back to your deathbed. If your life had not been a success, what's the second thing you would wish had happened that would have made it a success?"

I immediately knew what it was:

✦

I wish I'd said all the things I never got around to saying to my friends and extended family. I wish I'd confessed some secrets I was holding. I wish I'd told some people how much I loved and appreciated them. I wish I'd told my daughter how sad I felt that I'd broken some promises to her.

✦

Ed offered a summary: "You wish you'd completed a lot of big, significant communications to people you loved and cared about."

I nodded, dumbstruck at the weight of all the incomplete communications that tumbled through my mind. It seemed like I'd spent my whole life turning away from saying things that needed to be said. I saw the same pattern running throughout my whole family. We were masters of incompletion.

Ed saw my glazed-over look and snapped me out of it by saying, "No need to dwell on the negative. Just notice it and move on. When you see a wreck on the highway, there's no point in stopping to stare at it."

I got the point, and the fog lifted.

"Okay, turn that wish into a goal. Put it in the present tense," Ed said.

✦

My life is a complete success because I live in a state of completion with all my friends and family. I say all the important things I need to say, and do all the important things I need to do. As I go through life, there's nothing significant I leave unsaid or undone.

✦

Ed asked, "Why is that important to you?"

I told him I could feel the weight and pressure inside me of many incompletions with friends, family, and long-lost acquaintances. There were many things I'd left unsaid, many promises I'd broken, many amends I needed to make. I could feel the peace and clarity that would come from saying the things that needed to be said and handling the things I had left undone. At that moment I had no idea how I might go about completing all those things, but I knew I had to try.

He asked me to make a commitment to the goal.

As I committed to the goal, I felt again the sensation of energy and lightness in me, as if all the cells of my body were smiling at once.

He asked me what my third deathbed wish was. I was getting the hang of it now. I told him:

★

I wish I'd generated a complete written record of everything of significance I had learned during my time on earth.

★

My chosen path was as a teacher and writer, but at the time I did not feel I was teaching and writing about the things of greatest significance to me. I was still in the grip of the objective, scientific tradition of standing back and observing things from a distance, but I was feeling a deep urge to do a more personal kind of research. For example, nobody had ever explored the inner world of feelings from a scientific and personal perspective. I wanted to document my personal journey of learning, so that others who were interested might benefit from my experiences. Beyond that, though, I felt exhilaration at the thought of writing about the things that deeply mattered to me. I knew that I would die unfulfilled if I did not turn myself inside out and go to the limits of my creative ability.

"Great," Ed said. "Turn that wish into a right-now goal."

✦

My life is a success because I write about what is sacred to me. I generate an ongoing record of everything of significance that I learn.

✦

I could feel a powerful exhilaration glowing in my body the longer we talked. Ed was grinning from ear to ear, too. I noticed that a small group of people had gathered around, apparently attracted by the energy of the conversation.

"What's number four on your deathbed wish list?"

Now I was feeling so much in the flow that all I had to do was open my mouth and the words tumbled out.

I wish I'd developed an understanding of God and divinity — one that I could feel in my body, not just think about intellectually.

"Great," Ed said. "That was one of my deathbed wishes, too. Turn it into a goal."

I feel the presence of God all the time, everywhere I go. I know what divinity is and how the universe was created.

Ed nodded, as if this were the most ordinary request in the world. He asked me why this goal was important, and I explained that even as a child I had felt an almost allergic reaction to intellectual discussions of religion. I think some part of me knew about the destructive power of divisive beliefs, as well as the essential fruitlessness of mental concepts detached from direct experience.

"Is there a Number Five?" Ed asked.

There was.

✦

My life was not a total success because I rushed through it. I never stopped to savor the precious moments along the way.

✦

"Beautiful," Ed said. "Now, turn it into a goal."

✦

My life is a success because I savor every moment of it along the way.

✦

It was crystal clear to me why I wanted to enjoy the journey every step of the way. Growing up, I saw people all around me who were not having a good time. Some were slogging through life, just going through the motions, leading lives of quiet desperation. Others were suffering their way along, and many of those seemed to go out of their way to create their own suffering. I didn't want any part of that. I didn't yet know exactly what the meaning of life was, but I was fairly certain it wasn't "Get born, have a bad time, then die."

"Where are you with achieving each of those goals?" Ed asked.

I gave him my realistic appraisal: so far, my list was mostly just a bunch of good ideas.

He nodded. "That's where I was when I started."

I asked him to tell me more about his own deathbed experience. He said that as he lay there, not knowing if he would live or die, he found himself wishing he had done certain things that would have given his life meaning. He suddenly realized, though, that he was setting his standards far too low by merely wishing for a meaningful life. Why not wish for a magnificent life of complete fulfillment? He promised himself and God that if he were fortunate enough to live, he would devote his full energy to attaining the goals of greatness.

He recovered, and went on to complete them all successfully.

"That's why every time I get a chance, I ask everyone who looks like they have a spark of consciousness to figure out their deathbed goals."

We looked at each other in silence for a moment. There was nothing left to say. We shook hands, and he turned toward the door.

"Wait," I said. "Any last-minute advice for me?"

He gave me a wink. "Get busy."

I took that advice and got very busy, indeed.

In the pages that follow I tell you the story of how it all happened. In each of the first five chapters, I explore one of my wishes and the challenges I faced in making it come true. Between the first and second chapters I also tell you about a powerful lesson I learned — a piece of wisdom I've used to make every day of my life better for more than two decades since. The final chapter gives you a step-by-step guide to realizing your five wishes. There you'll find space to write down your wishes and explore why they're important to you. You'll discover what's been holding you back, and you'll learn how to create plans for making your wishes come true. Now, come with me on the journey of love that my first wish set in motion.

⋆

CHAPTER ONE

MY FIRST WISH

Lasting Love

Remember the first wish I made on my imaginary deathbed?

⋆

I wish I'd enjoyed a long and happy marriage with a woman I adored and who adored me.

⋆

WHY I WISHED FOR IT

At the moment I told Ed my greatest wish, I had no evidence that it was possible. I had never seen such a marriage. All I had to go on was a tiny glimmer of possibility that I could feel inside me. I also had the great gift of a new relationship with a willing partner, Kathlyn, who had the spirit of a true cosmic adventurer combined with a huge heart and a clear mind. I had never met anyone who had all the qualities I most desired in a woman. At the time, unfortunately, I was busily frittering away this big opportunity in the same way I'd messed up just about every relationship I'd ever been in: with indecision, lack of commitment, and an inability to keep my hands off other women.

My first love as a teenager was Alice, but even the glow of first love hadn't kept me from seeing Kathy and Joyce on the sly. Then came Linda, my first wife, and long before I left Linda, I was seeing Barbara and Jane. Then came Carol, who complained for five years that I was not committed to her. I strenuously told her how wrong she was, all the while enjoying wild, secret romps with Nancy, Donna, Barbara, and many others whose names I've forgotten. So when Kathlyn came along, offering me everything I'd ever dreamed of, my immediate response to this gift was to start seeing Lynne on the side.

So there I was, one foot in the relationship with Kathlyn, one foot out the back door. As soon as I formulated my first wish, I could feel this issue begin to seethe and ferment within me. I found myself asking, for the first time, why I persisted in splitting myself in half by pretending to be in one place while occupying another at the same time. Up until then I had never seen this dynamic as a pattern. I just thought it was the way life was supposed to be. Now suddenly I realized it was not only a problem — it was *the* problem.

One way a pattern stays hidden from oneself is through lack of awareness. But I had been going a step further to ensure that the pattern stayed in place. I'd added a drop of a superglue called self-righteous justification: I frequently proclaimed that monogamy was only for domesticated dull-ards, not for wild, free mavericks like me!

But suddenly this philosophy seemed hollow and false. Even worse, I was beginning to suspect that it was part of a hand-built defensive façade designed to hold me back from reaching a potential I deeply longed for. So, I asked myself, if my beliefs were indeed the problem, where had they come from? It only took a split second for the answer to become clear.

I had started out my life that way. I was literally born into the pattern.

My father had died shortly after I was conceived, so when I was born, my mother was both a grieving widow and an unemployed single parent. In desperate circumstances, she turned me over to my grandmother, who adored me and willingly took care of me. She had raised four daughters and had always longed for a son. At age sixty-five, she finally got her wish. But then my mother, out of guilt and her natural maternal urges, wanted me back, so back I went. Not long after, she changed her mind and returned me to my grandmother. For the next seven years, I shuttled back and forth between my mother and my grandmother in what was essentially a joint custody arrangement.

Yet it was my grandmother who felt to me like my real mother, whereas my mother was a person I visited from time to time. They lived down the street from each other, so if things became difficult with my mother — and they nearly always did — I could escape to the comfort of my grandmother's warm and loving presence. If I'd been given a choice, I would have probably never spent a single night at my mother's house. Ultimately, though, my mother insisted that I stay at her house permanently. After I started school there were fewer and fewer overnights at my grandmother's house. No wonder the thought of living with one woman now seemed like forced imprisonment!

The pattern was so obvious — why hadn't I seen it before I was in my thirties? I felt lucky I'd become aware of it, and at the same time embarrassed and stupid that I'd taken so long to see it.

HOW MY WISH CAME TRUE

*I'm enjoying a long and happy marriage
with a woman I adore and who adores me.*

I remember the exact moment when I realized the game was up — and that I was not going to spend the rest of my life playing out a destructive belief pattern created in childhood.

Not long after getting clear on my five wishes, I visited a friend and mentor of mine, Dwight Webb, at his place in New Hampshire. Kathlyn was in Colorado, where we both lived at the time. One day, I had Dwight's place all to myself while he was off teaching a class. As I strolled around the house, admiring the beautiful details of the cabin Dwight had built by hand, I had a sudden flash of insight: There was only one way I could find out if I had what it took to create the kind of relationship I really wanted. I had to make a deep, personal commitment to creating it — no matter what. The commitment had to be freely chosen by me, and it had to be large enough to include the likelihood that at some point in the process I would give up in despair when I confronted the biggest barriers to achieving my goal. My commitment needed to be powerful enough to get me through those barriers, and yet — this was the real kicker — there was no way to know what the barriers actually were until I made the commitment!

I made the commitment on the spot. Then I picked up the phone and called Kathlyn. I explained what I'd just realized, that I would never get to know whether the relationship of my dreams was possible until I made a whole-being commitment to it.

"I want to make a commitment to you, to create a passionate, creative lifelong relationship with you. Is this what you want?"

It was silent for a moment. Then I could hear quiet sobs over the phone. "Yes," she said at last.

I felt a deep smile spread through my whole body.

"Wonderful. I'm glad. I commit to creating this with you, and I commit to regarding anything I confront along the way — sexual feelings for other women, fear, despair, anything — as just stuff of mine that's coming up to distract me. I promise not to give up until we create the relationship of our dreams or we both agree to call off the quest."

"I make that promise to you, too," she said.

That conversation was more than a quarter-century ago, and everything I dreamed has come true. In fact, the fulfillment of my dreams has gone far beyond what I imagined was even possible. Along the way Kathlyn and I have raised two children to healthy adulthood, coauthored ten books, traveled widely teaching relationship seminars, faced the audience on *Oprah* and hundreds of other shows, weathered some hard times, and had many ecstatically good times.

Now, when people ask me if it's possible to feel lasting love, I can look them straight in the eye and say, "Yes." I know it can be done. I can give them not only hope and encouragement but also a realistic appraisal of the path — I know in my bones the attention it takes and the depth of commitment it requires.

And I can tell them it's worth every moment of careful attention it takes, because as I speak to them, I can feel the rewards of the quest: the glow of love and the calm of a heart in harmony with itself.

INTERLUDE
Then Along Came a Miracle

A miracle happened not long after I made my body-and-soul commitment to Kathlyn, and I believe the miracle was made possible by that deep commitment. As the love grew between us, we saw over and over that the power of commitment brings to the surface the deep fears, old wounds, and habit-patterns that need to be released in order to give and receive love fully in the present. In the process of making my first wish come true, I came face to face with a barrier that seemed insurmountable. In finding a way through this impasse, a breakthrough occurred that gave me a remarkable tool for transformation. It's a tool I've organized my life around ever since. I'd like to tell you what happened, so that you can understand the tool and put it to work for yourself.

When I had the conversation with Ed that started all this, I'd been involved for a couple of years in a struggle over a house. It was a house I didn't want but couldn't let go of. In fact, it was a house I'd never wanted to buy in the first place. Carol, the woman I was with at the time, had taken a major fancy to it, but I thought it was ugly and too expensive. I eventually gave in to her wishes, mainly because I wanted her to be happy. In those days I was under the woefully mistaken impression that things like real estate could make people happy. Later I would come to see that buying an ugly house I didn't want was a way to avoid facing an even uglier truth lurking inside me: I didn't want to be in the relationship anymore. Finally I left the relationship, but the house became a source of conflict that dragged on and on.

When Carol and I split up we had accumulated an amount of equity well over $100,000 in today's money. I wanted her to buy my half or sell the house so I could get my money out. She wanted to keep living in the house but only had $10,000 of the $50,000 she needed to buy me out.

Stalemate.

And so it dragged on for months, then a year. Each month I'd go through one of life's least fun experiences: having to make my half of the payment for a house I didn't like and didn't live in. I felt the pinch even more as my relationship with Kathlyn deepened. When we began living together, all we could afford was a tiny rental; from the moment we moved in, we couldn't wait to move out of it. The only person who seemed to be happy was Carol. She got to live in a house she liked and only had to pay for half of it! As time wore on, the minor satisfaction of making Carol happy dwindled and devolved into bitter envy.

Bitterness and envy were two emotions I hadn't spent much time feeling in my life, and I didn't wear them well. One day I was full of angry thoughts about Carol and the house, and to soothe my fevered mind I sat down to meditate. During meditation I was visited by a revelation. An image popped into my mind of a river flowing around a boulder. In that image was embedded a powerful insight: money is really only a form of energy. I realized that my attachment to "getting what I was entitled to" was a massive energy block, a boulder in the flow of my river. I was holding onto a house I didn't want until Carol came up with the full $50,000. By doing that I was blocking my own energy flow and, in a twisted sort of way, staying attached to Carol.

A radical question formed in my mind: What if I simply gave her my half of the house for whatever she could pay? I wondered if this act of giving would free up the energy flow, so that the money would come my way through some other means. It seemed like an outrageous idea when viewed through the filter of logic, but it seemed so intuitively right that I decided to act on it. Later that day I told Kathlyn what I'd realized.

She gulped when I told her I was going to let go of the house, because it represented my only tangible asset at the time. However, she immediately understood the money-is-energy insight and agreed that letting go of the house was the right way to go. I called Carol's attorney and asked him if she still had the $10,000. He said she did. "Okay," I said, "I'll give her my half for the ten grand."

"You will?"

He sounded astonished and skeptical.

"Yep," I said, "She likes the house and deserves to live in it. I'll make the $40,000 some other way."

He asked me what I meant, and I explained my insight about money and energy. He listened politely, although I imagine he thought I was either crazy or on drugs.

"I'll draw up the papers right away," he said.

Almost as soon as the ink was dry on the deal, I began to experience a new level of abundance in my life. A book contract came through, along with a substantial offer for a long-term consulting contract with (believe it or not) the U.S. Army. They wanted me to help bring innovative counseling to the staff of their drug and alcohol treatment programs. When all was said and done, I ended the year with well more than the $40,000 I'd given away in the house deal. Best of all, Kathlyn and I found a wonderful new home in the neighborhood we wanted to live in. All ended well for

Carol, too: she got married to a man who liked the house just fine.

The most important part for me was receiving the gift of a miracle that had lasting consequences in my life. In addition to understanding how the world of energy actually works, I also got a powerful tool for navigating through this new world. I learned that any significant incompletion acts like a boulder in a river. The river has to flow around it to get where it wants to go. One or two boulders may only hinder the flow, but pile up a few more and you start to dam the river. It doesn't take long for that dammed river to overflow its banks and get diverted toward a completely different destination.

The way to get the flow going in the right direction again is by completing any significant incompletion. The act of completing something, particularly if it has an emotional charge, is a remarkably powerful way to increase your abundance of love, money, health, and anything else that's important to you. You really have to see it and feel it to believe it, and that's what I'd like to explore with you next.

CHAPTER TWO

MY SECOND WISH

Completing

My second wish was all about completing —
tying up the many loose ends in my life. I soon
discovered a magical surprise: any significant act
of completion unleashes a hidden power, a rocket
fuel for manifesting your heart's desires. Every
time I completed anything that had an emotional charge, I liberated a new wave of energy
that increased my velocity toward my cherished
goals.

The dictionary says that *completion* is finishing
something and making it whole. I learned how
much of my energy and power was being con-
sumed by the things I'd left unfinished and un-
whole. I discovered how much energy, lightness,

and power I could feel by completing things and making them — and myself — whole. Here's how I first phrased my wish:

✦

I wish I'd said all the things I never got around to saying to my friends and extended family. I wish I'd confessed the secrets I was holding. I wish I'd told some people how much I loved and appreciated them. I wish I'd told my daughter how sad I felt that I'd broken some promises to her.

✦

Here's how I turned my wish into a goal:

✦

My life is a complete success because I live in a state of completion with all my friends and family. I say all the important things I need to say, and do all the important things I need to do. As I go through life, there's nothing significant I leave unsaid or undone.

✦

HOW IT WAS THEN

I come from a family of refugees and runaways. I had never seen this aspect of my lineage clearly until I formed my second wish. I chose this wish because I felt the pressure and weight of many things I'd run away from and left undone over the years.

As a kid, I lived near the railroad tracks, and I don't think I ever saw a train go by without wishing I could be on it. It wasn't until I was in my fifties that I found my true home, both inside myself and in the part of the world I live in. Before that, I'd always felt like I was on my way to someplace else — and the sooner, the better.

Once I began handling the many incompletions I'd left by the wayside in my past, I realized I had been following the well-worn patterns of a family script.

In doing some detective work on the pattern, I discovered that both my father and my maternal grandfather had run away from home when they were sixteen. Around 1890, my grandfather stole a mule from the family farm and rode off to seek his fortune in the newly settled territory of central Florida. The reason he always gave for his escape from the farm is both funny and insightful. "Farming," he would say, "will either kill you at a young age or make you tough enough to live to a ripe, old age. Death at an early age or a long life as a farmer seem about equal in my book." The clear message I took from this: If you don't like something, get out. Leave it behind and don't look back.

My father ran away from home by hopping a freight train. According to stories I heard from my mother, he had grown up in a terribly abusive family. His father "carried a Bible in one hand and a bullwhip in the other, and used them interchangeably." Finally one day he stowed away on a railway car, intending to take it from Alabama to Florida, but he got caught and thrown off the train. The same thing happened two or three more times, until finally the engineer gave him a job on the train as a locomotive stoker. In those days the steam engines ran on coal and sometimes wood;

the stoker's hot and dirty job was to watch the fire and keep it roaring. Although I never knew my father in the flesh, I saw many pictures of him wearing his striped railroad cap.

Going back even further, I'm descended from Protestants who were forced to flee parts of Europe because of the Huguenot persecutions of the eighteenth century. At one point, King Louis XV of France, a rabid Catholic, passed a law making it legal to persecute Protestants. Suddenly it was okay to steal from Protestants, even beat them on the street, with no punishment. This new law did not bring out the compassionate side of the Catholics, and many of the Protestants fled to England and other points west.

My European ancestors migrated to England and Scotland, and then came to America and took root in the South. They became successful in business and the plantation economy, only to find themselves on the losing side of the Civil War. They lost their lands and businesses, and fled farther south to start again in the jungles of Florida at the end of the nineteenth century.

Within this general refugee script were many smaller dramas that involved running away. My two aunts ran away from home to get married, in order to escape the wrath of my grandmother, who did not approve of the men they loved. Both of these marriages endured for more than forty years, during which time my grandmother forgave her two daughters but steadfastly refused to speak to their husbands. (You can see why Southerners tend to make such good novelists. All they have to do is write down what's going on around them.)

When I was nineteen, my grandfather, the former mule thief, slipped me $500 and told me to get the hell out of the swamplands before they swallowed me up. I took his advice, bought a beat-up '58 Ford for $175, pointed it north and never looked back.

Geographical liberation is one thing, but internal freedom is something else indeed. Escaping to New England and later to California changed the scenery but only reinforced my habit of not completing significant emotional communications.

By the time I was in my thirties and had my life-changing conversation with Ed, I had piled up such a stack of incomplete communications and unmade amends that I felt as though I was collapsing under the weight of them.

HOW IT IS NOW

One day, not long after my meeting with Ed, I sat down and made a list of all the incompletions I could think of. I broke them down into categories:

* Unspoken truths: Significant things I'd withheld from the significant people in my life.
* Broken agreements: Promises I'd made and hadn't kept
* People I appreciated and loved but hadn't told directly
* Money I owed

I wish I still had my original handwritten list, because I'm sure there were a few other categories I don't remember. The list was twelve pages long by the time I finished writing down all the things I'd left incomplete throughout my life. It seemed daunting when I looked at the list as a whole, but I was soon to discover something remarkable about the act of making completions: each one you take care of gives you a fresh burst of energy. If the completion is a major one, such as a big lie you finally admit to, the liberation of energy feels like rebirth.

The power of this phenomenon cannot be overstated. Why had I never heard of it before? Surely others must have tapped into the power of completion throughout history, but if they had, I certainly hadn't run across any descriptions of it. This discovery seems to me something that ought to be flashed across TV screens, awarded Nobel Prizes, and taught in every grade of school. Instead, I only learned it in my thirties, by a chance encounter with an esoteric teacher.

I set about the task of completing the incompletions, starting with the ones I felt most resistant to doing. I figured if I did the hard ones first, the easier ones would feel like eating dessert. The hardest ones were lies and broken promises to a number of women in my life, including my daughter and her mother, my long-ago first wife.

Linda and I were together for a little over four years, but they were probably the most unconscious four years of my life. I met and married her when I was twenty-two, just after my grandmother died. Looking back, I think I felt completely alone and without a source of love when my grandmother died. I remember just sitting in my backyard, for hours at a time, wondering what I was going to do with my life.

Linda strayed into my stagnant sludge-pond of grief, burdened by her own load of undigested feelings, and we stayed mired there for our short, unhappy time together. The only bright bit of sunshine to emerge from our union was our daughter, Amanda. Both of us adored her, and focusing our attention on our daughter enabled us to find some common ground between us. After a couple more years, though, we went our separate ways. Linda and Amanda moved a continent away, and I lost daily contact with Amanda. It was by far the most painful event of my life.

Several incompletions with Linda and Amanda

were at the top of my twelve-page list. I contacted Linda and asked her if she wanted to hear them. When she said yes, I got in the car and drove cross-country so I could sit down with her, and then with Amanda, face to face.

By then ten years had gone by since our divorce, but when Linda and I sat down together it was as if no time had passed. I told her about the process I'd gone through that had led me to make my list of incompletions. I asked her again if she wanted to hear them, and when she said yes, I began a sweaty but liberating hour of divulging secrets, feelings, and other unspoken pieces from our lives together.

I told her how angry I was that she had used Amanda as a pawn, punishing me by withholding visits for things she was mad at me for that were unrelated to Amanda.

I told her about a one-night stand I'd had, and the puny justification for it (retaliation for one I suspected her of having).

I expressed appreciation to her for taking care of Amanda by herself after our split-up.

I'm sure there were plenty of other things I

told her that day, but those are the ones I can remember now. People often ask me how to know whether an incompletion is significant enough to share with the other person. I use one main criterion for deciding if I should communicate it: is the other person likely to have an emotional reaction to it? If so, I definitely need to share it. If I think it's likely that the person will be angry or hurt or happy to hear it, I've found it's best to get it out into the light.

Knowing what to share with my daughter was more complicated. She was going through puberty at the time, and I knew she had enough on her mind. The major incompletions I had with her, though, seemed possibly useful to her in navigating the tricky passage she was going through. So I took the risk and asked her if she would sit down with me for a heart-to-heart talk. She agreed; we met at her favorite restaurant, and I told her my big ones.

I told her how guilty I felt about leaving her behind to be raised without my daily support. I told her it was the only major promise I'd ever broken, but it had pained me nearly every day of my life for almost thirteen years.

I told her I felt sad that on many occasions I'd expressed anger to her that was actually anger I felt toward her mother. As I spoke about this, I realized the same pattern had played out between my mother and me. She always seemed so angry with me, for reasons I could never figure out. Now it seemed to make sense: It was anger she felt toward my father but didn't know how to express. She must have been so furious at my father for dying young and leaving her in the lurch. She also must have felt afraid all the time. Taking care of a new baby is never easy, but being a poor widow in the backwoods of central Florida in the 1940s must have been especially hard. I felt a wave of compassion and forgiveness wash over me. Sitting in the corner of the restaurant, Amanda and I cried together and bonded in a way we hadn't in a long time.

Two of my incompletions required some detective work on my part, but the rewards were well worth the effort. In 1969 I'd borrowed $160 from my boss, so that I could take the one class I needed to finish my master's degree. I completed my degree, and had every intention of paying him back. Until, that is, we got into a big conflict. I resigned and took another job in another city. I refused to pay him back, using the justification that he was wrong, I was right, and therefore I didn't owe him anything. He made me angry; therefore I didn't owe him any money! Good thinking, Gay.

Justification is one of the glues that hold incompletions in place. In this case it took me close to fifteen years to unglue it. Until I made my twelve-page list, I had forgotten about the incident entirely. To make my list, I went back through my life year by year, and that's how I unearthed this debt from my memory.

I started looking for my old boss, finally tracking him down a few months later. He had fallen on hard times and was living in a tiny room in a YMCA. I wrote him a long letter, explaining the process I was going through and why I had tracked him down. I sent him the money, plus interest, and immediately felt a new sense of lightness and energy. He wrote back to tell me how flabbergasted he was to receive the money and how grateful he was. We wished each other well.

Next was my search for J. Wallace Hamilton. These were the days before computers and the Web. When I did a Google search for Dr. Hamilton recently, it took less than a second and yielded hundreds of pieces of information about him. But almost thirty years ago, the search took many phone calls, letters, and inquiries, but it finally paid off when I made contact with his widow in St. Petersburg, Florida.

J. Wallace Hamilton had delivered an inspiring talk at a Youth Day in the Methodist church I attended in high school. I was in a funk at the time, because I couldn't see any way out of the boxes I felt trapped in. Even if I escaped from the sweltering swamplands and rigid prejudices of the South of 1960, would I end up trapped in a white-bread suburb with a corporate job, a Betty Crocker wife, and 2.3 kids?

Then I heard Dr. Hamilton's talk, and it felt as

though he was speaking directly to me. The messages penetrated to my core:

* Don't settle for anything less than what you really want.
* Be wary about accepting offers of safety and security at the expense of your own creative freedom. Once you trade your freedom for the illusion of security, you have a hard time ever getting your freedom back.
* Follow your heart, and your life will be blessed with unexpected favors.

I made a secret pact with myself to follow his advice, and it served me wonderfully throughout the long, quirky, and often painful path to my own career. Now I realized I had never thanked him, and it felt like a huge incompletion.

After some searching, I finally found Mrs. Hamilton, Dr. Hamilton's wife. She told me he had died years earlier. As I told her my story, I got to experience the beautiful magic that often accompanies the act of completing significant communications. She told me that when my letter found its way to her, she was feeling depressed, wondering if her life — and her husband's — had meant anything. The timing of the letter was perfect for her.

Not only did I have the great pleasure of telling her how deeply his talk had affected me; I also discovered a treasure trove I'd never known about. Dr. Hamilton had written a number of books, long out of print, which Mrs. Hamilton offered to send me. Soon, I was holding in my hands the collected wisdom of J. Wallace Hamilton, a man whose twenty-minute talk had inspired me for life.

All these experiences gave me a reverence for the process of completing things. Part of the reverence came from the simple fact that completion feels good. On a daily basis I began to feel the inner peace that comes from taking care of big incompletions — such as clearing up a long-held resentment with a friend or family member — as well as the energy lift that comes from taking care of little incompletions such as making a phone call I've been putting off.

Feeling good is great, but there is a power to completion that goes beyond good feeling into the whole of life. What I've come to see is that the act of completing something, no matter how large or how small, puts you into harmony with the universe. If I say to you, "I'll call you today," I have created a new force in the universe, a new agreement about how things will be. If I then make good on my agreement and call you today, I line myself up in harmony with those forces. If I don't call you today, I leave a loose end, an open circuit, an unresolved story line. By not calling you, I communicate something that affects my life and our relationship: my word is no good, and you are not worth my effort to keep my word. My experience has been that each incompletion saps my energy and clouds my relationship with the people on the other end. The act of completion restores my energy and clears the air that circulates through my relationships.

Further, though, each act of completion celebrates our connection to the universe around us.

The universe becomes a friendlier place, because we're being friendlier to it. As I got better and better at completing things, I found the happy surprise of an unexpected reward: my path through the universe became smoother and easier. Daily life became blessed with positive coincidences both large and small. A long-forgotten loan to a friend was repaid, parking places appeared, Oprah read one of our books and invited us on her show. Things like these happened with greater and greater frequency as I honed the art of completion. Now, even though I've lived for many years on a steady diet of spontaneous positive events, I celebrate them every day and try never to take them for granted. I think of them as little winks from the universe. When they occur I give thanks for them, and wink back.

✦

CHAPTER THREE

MY THIRD WISH

Writing from the Heart

✦

*I wish I'd generated a complete
written record of everything of significance
I learned during my time on earth.*

✦

On the surface, my third wish might seem trivial in comparison to my first two wishes, but there was a big issue behind it that made it important to me. The issue really boiled down to this: Was I going to be real and honest in presenting to the world what I was most passionate about? Or was I going to spend my career hiding behind the safe wall of academic objectivity?

WHERE I BEGAN

As a professor of counseling psychology at the University of Colorado, my job was teaching graduate students the art and science of psychotherapy. In addition, I was expected to do academic research in the field. My dilemma was that I was beginning to think of therapy as more of a spiritual enterprise than a scientific one. I was exploring in intimate detail the inner world of emotion and spirituality as it unfolded in the healing process, and I did not see how the standard academic research tools could be applied. I was making fascinating discoveries that would eventually contribute to a broad movement that revolutionized the field, but at the time there was no precedent for this type of research. I was afraid that if I came right out and published my discoveries, I wouldn't get tenure and I'd be banished to academic Siberia. I enjoyed the prestige and perks of the university. Plus, there was a measure of family pride at stake — neither my parents nor my grandparents had attended college; members of the family considered my university professorship a feather in the family's cap. I didn't want to get thrown out the door so soon after gaining entrance to the party.

Yet making my third wish had made it clear to me what I had to do. I chose to put aside all my fears and commit myself wholeheartedly to the kind of up-close, personal work I cared about. I got a contract from a publisher to write a different kind of book about self-esteem, one in which I would examine the subject from inside myself, with no other microscope but the light of my own consciousness. It was titled *Learning to Love Yourself,* and from the moment I began to write it, my life was never the same.

Although I had published several other books, this was the first one I felt passionate about writing. I poured my heart and soul into every sentence. Instead of writing with thoughtful distance and careful analysis, the style I was steeped in as a result of my Stanford PhD training, I hurled myself into the maelstrom of my own confusion, anxieties, and joys. I described as intimately as I could all the ecstasies and agonies that gripped me. My only criterion was truth. At the end of a sentence I would pause and ask myself, *Is that absolutely, unarguably true?* If I got a clear Yes, I went on to write the next sentence. When I finished the book, I felt for the first time in my career that I had fulfilled my creative potential.

The book changed my life in many other ways, some of which took me by surprise and spun me in unfamiliar directions. When the book hit the streets in the early eighties, it was subjected to a scathing review in a popular magazine, *Psychology Today*. However, through the sweetest of ironies, this awful review led to a wonderful outcome.

Self-help books were fairly rare in those early days, and to my knowledge there had never been one in which the author revealed his or her own feelings to the extent that I did in this book. It was this deeply personal aspect that so outraged the *Psychology Today* reviewer, R. D. Rosen.

A friend called me one Sunday afternoon. "Have you seen the new *Psychology Today*?" he asked.

"No," I said. "Why?"

"Do yourself a favor," he said. "Don't read it." He said that the review of my new book wasn't exactly flattering and that I was probably better off not burdening myself with the details.

Now I was really curious. I seldom read *Psychology Today*, but based on my friend's tantalizing warning I just had to rush down to the nearest newsstand to get it. I didn't even wait to purchase the magazine, so eager was I to devour the forbidden fruit. I stood by the magazine rack and flipped through the pages until I came to the review. It was then that I learned of the pain and suffering I had inflicted on R. D. Rosen.

Rosen not only hated the book (and the emerging self-help genre in general), but he intimated that I had lost my mind and sacrificed my academic reputation by sharing my own feelings of anger, anxiety, and longing. He even shared some feelings of his own, saying that parts of my book were so personal that they made him sick to his stomach! (I heard later that Rosen was a part-time restaurant critic. In that line of work, saying something makes you sick to your stomach is probably the harshest criticism of all.)

My own stomach wasn't in the best shape by the time I finished reading the review. I slunk back to my house feeling as though a hit-and-run driver had run over my career.

What had I done? Here I was, a professor at a major university. I had written many articles in scientific journals, plus a textbook in my field of counseling/clinical psychology. Now, R. D. Rosen was using my book as an example of the decline of academia and Western civilization in general. He and I were definitely on different wavelengths. Although I had my beefs with the university, I loved it and the rigorous, free inquiry it stood for. I just didn't think that a number-based, objective research style applied to my field. Teaching graduate students in a counseling psychology program was something I loved to do, and I felt I had a way of bringing a much-needed wave of authenticity and emotional expression to the academic world. The harsh reality, however, was that the *Psychology Today* review would likely be read by more people than had read my textbook and all my scientific articles combined. Was I going to become a laughingstock?

Now for the sweet irony: After the *Psychology Today* review came out, my book took off like a rocket. Sales doubled the next month, and then tripled the month after that. I discovered the truth of the old adage "There's no such thing as bad publicity." Apparently, the reading public liked the very things that had turned the reviewer's stomach. I began to get tearful letters of appreciation from people who thanked me for baring my soul, saying that the book had healed them by giving them permission to bare theirs. I received letters from other professors saying that I'd restored their faith in the academic world and given them a reason to go on teaching. The book became a steady bestseller, going through more than twenty printings over the next two decades.

The best was yet to come: After the book became a bestseller, I was inundated with requests to do talks and seminars. I fell into a pattern of teaching all week at the university and then flying off somewhere to do a talk or seminar on the weekend. One winter a few years later, I flew to Hawaii to teach a seminar. I got off the plane and stood on the tarmac luxuriating in the 80-degree warmth of Kauai. Moments later my hosts handed me a message from my secretary back in Colorado. "Urgent," the note said. "Oprah Winfrey called."

There was a long stretch of my life when I did not own a TV, so I was way out of touch with the goings-on of the popular media. I called my secretary to find out who this Oprah Winfrey was and why it was so urgent. According to my secretary, who faithfully devoured *People* magazine each week, Oprah was an up-and-coming talk show host in Chicago who was starting to get national attention. She wanted to do a show on the theme of *Learning to Love Yourself*. Was there any possibility I could turn around and come back to Chicago to appear on her show?

It was winter, and I had just escaped the frozen steppes of Colorado to enjoy a week of Kauai sunshine. I pondered the idea of taking a ten-hour flight back to the Midwest. My pondering lasted about two seconds. I told my secretary to decline. Later that day, I visited the author Shakti Gawain's house on Kauai and discovered that Shakti had appeared on *Oprah* and sold hundreds of thousands of books as a result. Suddenly winter and Chicago seemed a lot more appealing. However, I resisted the temptation and stuck with my decision to stay in Hawaii. Apparently, declining the offer did not terminally offend Oprah's producers, because later they were kind enough to have both Kathlyn and me for several appearances. We were blessed with great book sales, but the appearances on *Oprah* and other shows led to something far more rewarding: the founding of our own institute.

WHAT EMERGED

As a result of the increased visibility, we got requests from hundreds of therapists, MDs, and other professionals who wanted to study with us. Soon, we were offering training seminars in North

America, Asia, and Europe to accommodate those requests. The Hendricks Institute has grown over the past twenty years to become a thriving training center, graduating several hundred professionals a year. We also offer seminars to growth-oriented laypersons; about 20,000 people have participated over the years.

I can trace all of this to the choice I made to step out from behind the "Tweed Curtain" of academic respectability and venture into the pathless land of authentic expression. That journey took me backward in time, to examine my earlier work in the light of the new insight, and it took me forward in time to right now, serving as a navigational tool all the way.

First, I went back through the notes and notebooks I had kept since my entry into the counseling profession in 1968. I evaluated everything in light of these kinds of questions: *Have I used this to change my own life and/or have I personally seen it change someone else's life?* or *Is this something I merely think might be true and useful because I read about it, heard about it, or got it in some other indirect way?*

Over time, I shortened these questions to: *Is it true? Does it work? Have I personally used it to change my own life?* Ever since, these questions have been my acid test for determining whether something is worth writing about.

The questions have also steered me to one important personal insight after another. One of the biggest insights led to the body of relationship work Kathlyn and I have created. It started when we noticed a troublesome pattern in the early days of our relationship. We would be close for a few days, and then something would happen that would cause us to lose the flow of close connection. We would have an argument or get sick or get caught up in a family drama with our children or in-laws. Then it would take us days or weeks to get back into the flow of connection again. One day I had an awareness that helped us break through the pattern.

I was doing some stretching exercises upstairs in our house, on a clear, sunny morning in Colorado. I was feeling that easeful inner glow many of you are probably familiar with if you've done yoga or some other body-centered practice. Suddenly I went from feeling the delicious feeling to worrying about my daughter, Amanda, who had gone away to boarding school for the first time. The good feeling in my body disappeared as my mind began to manufacture scenes of her feeling lonely and homesick, being picked on by other students, and so on. None of these images had any reality to them; in other words, she hadn't told me of any such negative experiences, or indeed any negative experiences at all.

I went into the bedroom to call her and find out if she was okay. Then suddenly I stopped in my tracks as a realization gripped me: What if the good feeling itself had given rise to the scramble of anxious thoughts that had flooded my mind? Did I have an upper limit of how good I could let myself feel before bringing myself back down? Did I have an arsenal of strategies — arguments, worry thoughts, illness — that I unconsciously used to bring myself down when I exceeded my thermostat setting for how good I could let myself feel?

This awareness brought a flood of new possibilities into my mind. Maybe a lot of the arguments, upsets, and other unpleasant events didn't have anything to do with the events themselves — they were all just ways we blocked the flow of good feeling and love. But why? Why would we stop ourselves from feeling good? The answers jumped into my mind: Because we didn't think we deserved to feel good. Because we didn't think we deserved to feel love. And, perhaps most important, we sabotaged our good feeling because we simply didn't have much practice feeling good for any substantial length of time. The history of humanity, as well as our personal histories, teaches us a lot about adversity and how to deal with it but very little about how to feel good and maintain that feeling.

Wow! I felt electrified by this awareness, but before I rushed down to tell Kathlyn about it, I called my daughter to do a reality check. It turned out she was happily playing soccer. Her residence hall counselor (who apparently had considerable practice in dealing with overanxious parents) kindly looked out her window and described my daughter's enthusiastic soccer play. I thanked her and went downstairs to tell Kathlyn about the insight. She immediately saw the possibilities, and we began observing our patterns more closely over the following weeks and months. Once we knew what we were looking for, the pattern became plain as day. Almost all our conflicts, it turned out, occurred on Fridays or Sundays. Looking more closely, we realized that our Friday conflicts often came out of feeling the sweet end-of-the-workweek relief. Apparently we didn't have much tolerance for that feeling, because we would often get into conflicts after feeling it for an hour or so. The Sunday conflicts seemed to come in the late afternoon or evening after a period of closeness earlier in the day.

Once we got skilled at noticing the pattern, we found it possible to stay close for longer and longer periods of time. It took a lot of awareness, though, and it was definitely not an overnight process. I can't count the number of times we'd catch ourselves drifting into conflict and say something like, "Are we trying to mess up our intimacy by picking a fight right now?" Gradually, we were able to stay in the flow of intimacy for weeks and then months without creating a disturbance to stop it. We became able to stay in the flow even when we were handling challenges, like one of us wrecking the other one's car, family dramas, and the ultimate test: the remodeling of a hundred-year-old Victorian home. As of this writing, it has been well over ten years since either of us has spoken a cross word or even a critical word to the other.

All our relationship books — from *Conscious Loving* through five more books spanning nearly twenty years — came from writing about things that were kitchen-tested in our own relationship before we started using them with our clients. They were all written with variations of those key questions in the backs of our minds — *Is it true? Does it work? Have we personally found it to increase the flow of love and intimacy?*

By living in these questions my third deathbed goal — writing from the heart about everything significant I've learned during my time on earth — has been achieved, and continues to be achieved, beyond anything I ever imagined.

✦

CHAPTER FOUR

MY FOURTH WISH

Feeling God

"What's this God stuff all about?"

According to a family story, this question sprang from my lips when I was a pre-schooler. If the story is true, it means I've been trying to get God on the line for most of my life. Whenever my interest started, it was still burning in me when Ed asked about my deathbed wishes and goals. When he asked me to look back over my life from the un-fulfilled perspective, I phrased my wish like this:

✦

I wish I had developed an understanding of God and divinity, one that I could feel in my body, not just think about intellectually.

✦

With Ed's assistance I turned my wish into a present-tense goal:

✦

I feel the presence of God all the time, everywhere I go. I know what divinity is and how the universe was created.

✦

WHO I WAS

For me it was all about feeling the presence of God. One of the things that most bothered me about church when I was a kid was the lack of feeling. Everybody looked bored and dutiful while the minister droned on and on. At the other extreme were the Holy Rollers. In the part of the South I grew up in there were literally dozens of small denominations, each with its own special way of worshipping. Two blocks away from the house I grew up in, a tiny Holy Roller church came to life every Sunday. On a hot day they would leave the doors open during the service. Their shouts and screams and other "joyful noise" sometimes got so loud that we would close our doors and windows in spite of the heat. One time I strolled by slowly during their service, so I could see what was going on. People were wailing and jumping around while an organ and a drummer blasted away in the background. The minister was up front, pumping his fists toward the ceiling with his eyes rolled back in his head. The whole scene looked crazy to me.

I remember thinking: *If the choice is between bored and crazy, I guess I'll take bored.* Inside me, though, I knew I'd never be satisfied until I got a taste of the real thing. I didn't know at the time that it would take twenty years or more of searching until I finally found the experience I was looking for.

WHAT I BECAME

After my conversation with Ed, I finally began to have the kind of rich experiences I'd yearned for as a child. The experiences grew more and more frequent, and now they're a regular feature of my life. I began practicing meditation every day, and I believe it was that regular practice that opened the space in me for deep, direct experiences of the Divine. My first experiences of meditation came by way of the Zen Buddhist tradition, using their technique of breath-counting. Although I found a measure of stillness with Zen meditation, I also found it somewhat dry and hard. The teacher recommended at least two hour-long sessions a day, a schedule that was difficult to integrate into my life. In 1973 I discovered Transcendental Meditation (TM), and it was through this beautiful practice that I began to feel the presence of God on a regular basis. The TM techniques use mantras, which I found much more soothing to my system than the breath-counting techniques of Zen. The practice, with its two 20-minute sessions a day, was also much easier to work into my busy life.

I went on to learn a number of the advanced techniques taught through the TM organization. All of them were excellent and produced the results they promised: increased peace and harmony inside, along with increased productivity outside.

The practice became an essential feature of my daily life, just like taking a shower or brushing my teeth — perhaps even more essential, because while I've skipped a shower on occasion, I haven't missed a day of meditation since 1973.

I believe that practicing meditation gradually created an openness in me, an inner willingness that invited the powerful experiences that made my fourth wish a reality. Here's an example of one of those experiences.

It happened one bright spring morning in Colorado as I was walking across a college quadrangle. It was spring break, and all was quiet except for the crunch underfoot of light snow from the night before. I had just been browsing in a bookstore and had leafed through a book of phrases that Jesus had spoken. Now, as I was walking home, I began to think of the amazing paradox inherent in Christianity and other religions. Jesus had talked about love and brotherhood, but his followers had slaughtered millions in various crusades and sectarian squabbles. He had delivered a message of liberation, but it had given rise to an organized church that was monstrously oppressive, especially to women. It was a message of compassion and tolerance, but his followers could twist it to mean that it was okay to spit on women entering an abortion clinic. How could such a distortion have happened?

As I pondered this question I began to see through the words and concepts about Jesus and Christianity. Words can cause conflict; people can argue for centuries about concepts. But underneath all the words and argument there must be something essential and pure and true. I began to wonder: What is the *experience* that underlies it all? Maybe the experience is so strong that people can only handle a little bit of it before they withdraw from it into the world of words, concepts, and conflict. Maybe the actual genuine experience is so powerful it makes some people crazy. At the other extreme, people withdraw into boredom because they fear the power of the experience.

It suddenly occurred to me that Jesus might have tapped into a primal power source, a level of consciousness available to everyone. Certainly, Jesus had alluded to this often enough, in phrases like "Seek ye the kingdom of heaven within." Perhaps the Christ consciousness exists like a channel on a television set, ready to be tuned into by anyone who chooses to turn the dial to that channel. In that moment I decided to tune in. I stopped in my tracks, right there in the middle of the quadrangle. I let go of the thoughts in my mind and said something like this to myself: *Okay. I'm available. Show me.*

The next moment a powerful wave of energy rolled through my body, filling me with an electric feeling of exhilaration. It was a sweet feeling of heat and light, and it ricocheted up and down and around my body. Suddenly the sweet heat and light seemed to center in my heart, and I felt a boundless compassion for all humankind. My heart felt like it was cracking open, with love and gratitude to everyone pouring out. I saw all the earth and heavens as one big Being. There was no separation among all beings, all nature and myself — all were equal and one. We were all together in a dance of love and celebration. I remember turning slowly around in circles looking at the sky and the trees and the people I could see in the distance. We were all one thing, connected by a quantum field of love and compassion. All of us shared our divinity.

After a few minutes the intensity of the feeling began to ebb, and I headed homeward with a light step and a big smile. In the coming days I found that some conflicts I had with other people seemed to clear up effortlessly. I think this happened because I'd seen that we were all one. Once I realized that all of us were expressions of a central creative force in the universe, I found it hard to hold on to an adversarial position with people around me.

A few months later I had an experience in which I felt directly plugged into Divinity at an even deeper level. One August night I was lying down after a meditation. (It was my custom to lie down for ten or fifteen minutes after completing my evening meditation. The period of postmeditation rest feels particularly delicious because it allows the body to rest while the mind is quiet.)

As I relaxed in the silence I began to speculate about who or what God really was. I was thinking that practically nothing we are taught about God has any value; it is all based on someone else's experience, if in fact it is based on experience at all. I saw that what we're taught about God usually prevents us from inquiring into ourselves deeply enough to have a personal experience of God. In addition, the information we get about religion is usually dispensed by organized churches with ulterior motives.

We are usually taught to acknowledge God as a force outside ourselves, as the creative force in the universe, and ourselves as something created by God. On the other hand, many mystics — including Jesus — teach that we and God are one and the same. How can we be the creator and the created at the same time? I started to fog over with confusion at trying to sort this out with my mind. Suddenly, though, I saw a glimmer of light at the end of this conceptual tunnel. Perhaps somewhere behind all the twisted misinformation about God is a real experience that could be tapped. After all, if I could experience myself as something created by God, it made sense that I could follow the chain of creation back to the source.

I started with what was real and unarguable, by becoming aware of myself as a human. I felt my body sensations, my anger, my fear, and my happiness. I acknowledged my mind, with all its doubts and memories and ideas. I spent several minutes claiming and accepting all of the human aspects of myself. Then I let myself open up further, becoming willing to experience myself as the creator of all that.

Suddenly an explosion of light and vibration occurred deep inside me. I began vibrating intensely, shaking so fast and hard that it flipped me around on the bed. Although it might sound frightening, it actually felt completely benign. I felt as if a powerful current was coursing through me, like a clean river of energy. I stayed with the feeling for a long time, breathing into it rather than resisting it. When I breathed with it and surrendered to it, I could feel the currents pulsing even stronger through me. After a half hour or so the vibrations subsided, and I lay there feeling a delicious sensation of space and ease in my body. A thought floated into my mind: "So that's what God is. It's not something you think, it's something you feel."

No wonder I had never been able to figure it out with my mind. God was an experience, not a concept. God was, in the best sense of the word, *unthinkable*. I took the cue, and began to put my attention on *feeling* God instead of thinking about God. Gradually over the past thirty years the feeling of God has gone from being a fleeting momentary experience to something I sense in the background of my daily life almost all the time.

This awareness came in waves of deeper discovery. I found that I could feel a sensation of spacious ease everywhere I placed my attention in my body. For example, if I felt some tension in my shoulders, all I had to do was rest my attention on the feeling of tension for a few seconds. Soon, the tension would disappear and I would become aware of a sweet sensation of ease and space in the background of where the tension had been. At first I thought perhaps the easeful spacious sensation was there because the tension had melted. With more sensitivity, though, I found something very different to be true. The spacious, easeful feeling was there all the time, even when I felt tense (or achy or hungry). I just hadn't noticed it because I was focused on the foreground sensation of the tension (or hunger). Soon, I was looking for the sweet, spacious, easeful feeling everywhere in my body, and wherever I looked, there it was.

In time, I could feel more dimensions of this sensation. As I paid more attention to it, I found that it gave me a sense of connection with other people. In other words, as I grew more aware of it inside me, I felt its presence in other people, too. I liked the feeling of unity this awareness gave me as I moved through the world. At first, I wondered if this was a figment of my imagination or if other people were aware of it, too. To answer this question, I began to do some simple experiments in seminars and counseling sessions. If clients mentioned they were tired or had a headache, for example, I would invite them to place attention on the sensations of the headache or fatigue. Then, I would invite them to keep resting their attention on the unpleasant sensations until they noticed the sensations beginning to change. I invited them to notice if there were other background sensations they could feel in and around and behind the fatigue or headache. Sometimes it took a few seconds and sometimes a few minutes, but inevitably they would become aware of the sensations of spacious ease and flow. They would almost always experience an eyes-widening "Aha!" of discovery when their awareness expanded into the new sensation.

Initially I called this sensation "pure consciousness." Then one day a student in one of my seminars referred to it as a feeling of "organic divinity." She said it was like the feeling she had in church when she was child. She went on to say that this feeling had gone away as she got more wrapped up in the theology and dogma of the religious teachings. She was excited to discover that the feeling was still there and didn't depend on the particular teachings of the church. This led to an exciting discussion in which other students agreed with her and chimed in with their experiences. Their conclusion was that the sensation I'd been calling "pure consciousness" was the natural spiritual essence all of us came into life with.

That works for me, but I'll leave it to you to find out for yourself whether it feels like "organic divinity" or "pure consciousness." Ultimately, it may not matter what we call it. What matters most to me are feelings of connection to myself and other people and the universe around me. What's important to me now are the moments of ordinary life that are made extraordinary through feeling a unity of consciousness that connects us all. As that feeling happened more and more often, I realized that my fifth wish was coming true.

CHAPTER FIVE

MY FIFTH WISH

Savoring Life

When I made my fifth wish, I was feeling sad about all the times I'd hurried and hustled my way through things that later I wished I'd savored. Up until my conversation with Ed, no matter where I was, I always felt I should be somewhere else. The watch on my wrist ruled my world, and it was always telling me I should be a few minutes ahead of wherever I was. That's why I said to Ed:

My life was not a total success because I rushed through it. I never stopped to savor the precious moments along the way.

93

When Ed asked me to turn it into a goal, I said:

✦

My life is a success because I savor every moment of it along the way.

✦

ALWAYS ELSEWHERE

At the time I formed this wish, I'd just had an experience of myself at my worst with regard to this trait. My daughter had spent hours constructing an elaborate Halloween costume. She had constructed out of cardboard a perfect replica of a corrugated metal trashcan. She spray-painted it green, to match the color of the cans that lined our street on trash pick-up day. She wore the can around her, and the lid served as her hat. The liner was made of a plastic trash bag, which she had also crafted into suspenders that held the can in place. Around the outside of the can she had stenciled "Candy Disposal Unit." Her costume was the receptacle into which people could throw their candy, and before the evening was over she could hardly stagger along, so heavy was her load. My description does not do justice to its quirky creativity or the hilarious effect it had on people who saw it. As I took her from house to house trick-or-treating, her costume caused a stir every time someone opened the door to us. Usually the reaction was along the lines of, "Hey, honey, you've got to come see this!"

Yet instead of savoring this evening of home-made performance art, I found myself getting impatient after she visited just a few houses. I had other things to do — a speech I was working on, a backlog of phone calls to return. I began to give her "hurry-up" signals, and soon, to please me, she was virtually sprinting from house to house. When we returned home we were both exhausted.

After I put her to bed I started to work on my speech but then realized I was so tired I couldn't think straight. What had I hurried for? Why had I rushed through such a sweet evening to get back to work? And now the rushing had wiped me out so I couldn't even work. I felt disgusted that I'd missed another magic moment of Amanda's child-hood. Sadly, it hadn't been the first.

I could feel the pinch of this issue on the personal level, in my relationship with Amanda, but I could also feel the spiritual consequences of hurrying through life. I was beginning to understand why the world's spiritual traditions stressed the value of being in the moment, celebrating the present, and living in the now. The magic of life happened in the now. The present was where the holy moments of life occurred, whether they were exalted peak experiences or the simple joys of holding a child's hand while she trick-or-treated.

When I formed my fifth deathbed wish, my life was about 10 percent as busy as it is today. However, it's been a long time since I've felt rushed or hurried or pinched for time. Somewhere along the way I learned to take it easy even as life sped up. Learning to savor the moments of life is an ongoing process, so I hope I'll always be learning to savor more and more. For now, though, I feel an immense satisfaction at how far I've come.

It seems like a miracle, to go in one lifetime

from always wanting to be someplace else to always feeling there's no place I'd rather be. It happened not in a flash of enlightenment but in hundreds of moments of catching myself being somewhere else, then bringing myself back to the present. Here's one I remember: standing in the cold watching my daughter's fifth-grade soccer team being mercilessly drubbed by their crosstown rivals. I had a pounding headache, exacerbated by the screaming parents all around me. My mind was full of fantasies of things that could only be obtained elsewhere: steaming cups of coffee, my fireplace, a mystery I was reading. Then I caught myself "vacating the premises" and brought myself back to the moment. In the moment I was still cold and miserable, but I could also feel why I was there. I was there to be with Amanda, to share her life, to love and support her through glorious victory and merciless drubbing. Later, walking toward the car arm-in-arm with her, applying a bandage to a skinned knee, suggesting a trip to the pizza parlor for her and her best friend — that was one of the moments that give life its radiant glow.

If I'm not present during those moments, I'm not showing up for my life. No show, no glow: those seem to be the rules. Gradually, I caught myself in the act of vacating the premises enough times that I broke the habit. I began to show up where I was more and more. Being right there became the habit, then the preference, and ultimately an ongoing celebration. To illustrate this part of the story, I'd like to share two of those precious moments with you.

NOWHERE BUT HERE

The first moment took place during a bicycle trip I took in Tibet in 1986. It involves a visit to a fabled monastery. The second moment, no less sacred to me, happened while I was biking in Italy and involves a bowl of soup. I fell in love with bicycles when I was a kid and have logged thousands of miles on bikes as a grown-up, so it's appropriate that both of these moments took place on bike trips.

Floods had wiped out some of the road between

Lhasa and Shigatse, the second-largest city in Tibet and home of the Tashilumpo monastery. We ended up putting the bikes on the back of a big truck that dropped us off at the top of a 17,000-foot pass about fifty miles from Tashilumpo. After an hour of getting organized at the top of the pass (and feeling drunk as a result of the thin air at that height) we mounted our bikes and set off toward Tashilumpo monastery. The first hour of the journey was one of the most exhilarating rides of my life — downhill all the way to 12,000 feet on a twisting gravel road, a road with thousand-foot drop-offs and not a single railing! Fortunately, we all got to the flatland intact, and we paused briefly to celebrate at the side of one of the most beautiful lakes I've ever seen.

The rest of the journey was a different story. We rode up and down dozens of hills, twenty-some miles of pedaling into a stiff wind at 12,000 feet. The physical challenge was more intense than anything I'd ever experienced. I was around forty years old at the time, in pretty good shape for someone my age. That ride, though, pushed me to my edge. A couple of the riders were hardy twenty-somethings who outdistanced the rest of us by a few miles. The rest of us spread out pretty much according to age, with the riders in their sixties bringing up the rear a couple miles behind.

As the wind got stronger, so did my determination to get to Tashilumpo. Soon I was pedaling in first gear at about two miles per hour, at the very limit of my body's strength. At one point my physical exhaustion got to such a point that I started hallucinating about my grandmother. She had been dead for twenty years, but I somehow got the impression that if I got to Tashilumpo I could see her again. My efforts became frantic in my push to hurry up so I could get there quicker.

Eventually, though, I understood the true nature of this fantasy. It didn't have anything to do with getting to Tashilumpo. I realized it was really about opening up to my love for my grandmother and my grief about her absence from my life. I opened my mouth to the wind and my heart to the sadness I felt. I felt like I was carrying out a ritual of purification. I was being cleansed of something old so that something new could live and breathe inside me. Now I was gasping massive breaths of air in and out as I pedaled along, sobbing uncontrollably about my grandmother's love that I would never feel again. I could feel part of me wanting to resist the pain of those feelings and push them out of my awareness, but in that moment I remembered my wish to savor every moment of life. Instead of pulling away from the feelings, I abandoned myself to them fully, savoring the grief of missing her, the joy of having known her, and the blessing of her love.

And at the peak of my straining, just when I thought I couldn't go any farther without collapsing, I felt the blossoming of a new awareness inside me. A powerful realization welled up from within: at the deepest level of myself I *am* my grandmother's love. There is no way I can lose her love, not ever — it is in every cell of my being. My grandmother's love lives in me, and I live in it. It isn't going anywhere — it is here for all time.

At that point, a seeming miracle happened in

the outside world. The wind, which had been in my face for the past hour, suddenly shifted to my back as I pedaled around a curve in the road, and suddenly I was flying along at twenty miles an hour rather than creeping along at two. My breath was still rushing powerfully in and out of my lungs, but now it came and went freely in the huge open space that had been cleared of my ancient grief. I flew down the road, celebrating with great gasping lungfuls of pristine air.

In the distance, I saw small dwellings signaling the outskirts of the town. I rode in standing up on my pedals, waving at monks and kids who waved back with radiant smiles on their faces.

I found my way through the back streets, guided by kids pointing the direction, and braked to a stop at the gates of Tashilumpo. The journey was over. I was there.

And now, for another form of savoring, I'd like to offer you a celebratory taste of soup. Please turn on your imaginary taste buds to enjoy with me a moment I've treasured for many years:

One day in northern Italy, as Kathlyn and I rode our bicycles along a country road, I started fantasizing about having a bowl of minestrone for dinner. We were cold and exhausted and had far to go, so we began using the minestrone as a motivator. Every few miles one of us would call out, "Tell me about the minestrone!" If I were doing the description, I'd spin a loving tale about the richness of the broth, the perfection of the spices, the freshness of the tomatoes, the warmth of the fireplace in front of which we'd be served, and any other detail that would help the miles go by. When it was Kathlyn's turn, she'd take the minestrone into some higher stratosphere of magnificence. On we went, heads bent into the wind, driven forward by our quest for the ultimate minestrone. We used the imaginary savoring of the soup as another way to savor the right-now experience of being on our bikes. "My shoulders ache," I'd call over to Kathlyn as we huffed up some long hill. "Imagine feeding them a spoonful of the minestrone," she'd call back. "Feel it warming and soothing all those achy places."

Finally, in late afternoon we pedaled slowly into the town of Alba. As we cruised down the main street, we searched right and left for the restaurant that would serve us the yearned-for soup. We passed one restaurant that looked absolutely perfect, but our pounding hearts sank when we saw that it wouldn't be open for an hour. Another one loomed up on the right. It looked wonderful, but the proprietors were just setting out the tables. Not open yet. By now we were nearly in tears.

Suddenly fate or intuition or just good luck intervened. We got the impulse to veer down a little side street. There, halfway down the block, was the restaurant of our fantasies, *and the door was open!* We screeched to a halt and practically fell over each other to get in the door. We were greeted by a wonderful aroma of garlic, bread baking, and chickens roasting.

But no! The staff members were all seated around a large table, having their own meal. They looked up at us, two alien intruders, and we realized we'd forgotten to remove our helmets. The headwaiter, who turned out to be the only one who spoke any English, came to us and humbly apologized that they were not quite open. "Give us just a half an hour," he said. "We are having our simple meal."

We looked longingly at their "simple meal." You can probably guess what it was — a vast serving bowl of minestrone, accompanied by freshly baked loaves of bread. Several of the staff were so caught up in their enjoyment of it that they didn't even look up from their bowls.

We stared at the soup, entranced. We wanted it. We wanted it badly. We wanted it now.

Somehow we must have transmitted the depth of our forlornness to the headwaiter, because he stepped back and regarded us compassionately. He held a finger aloft, then had a rapid-fire conversation with the staff, apparently appealing to them about our plight. He turned to us and said, "All we can offer you at the moment is our minestrone, but maybe it will make you happy until our chef can finish his meal." He lowered his voice gravely, "If he does not eat, he cannot cook."

We practically wept with gratitude. We bowed, we blew them kisses, we staggered to a table and removed our helmets and gloves. Soon two large bowls of the minestrone were set before us with a flourish. A loaf of heaven-sent bread came next, along with two glasses of ruby-red wine. We thanked him profusely and took spoons in hand.

For the next half hour a soup celebration was held in Alba. And what a soup it was! This was soup raised to the level of a sacrament. I kept asking Katie questions like "What is that spice?" and "How did they get tomatoes to taste like this?" Needless to say, it measured up to all our fantasies and then some. When our bowls were empty we looked up at each other and made a decision: the quest would end here. We resolved never to order minestrone in a restaurant again. This was it.

It's been many years since that day in Alba, but several times each winter I'll drop a broad hint or two to my master-chef wife. "Katie," I'll say. "Remember the Alba minestrone? Remember how wonderfully deep and hearty that broth was? Remember the way the beans were perfectly cooked and how it had those tiny bits of lean bacon in it? Remember how that soup seemed to nurture our very souls?" A dreamy look will come over her as the memory takes hold. Next day, or maybe the day after that, I'll come into the kitchen and my nose will be greeted with the heady aroma of minestrone cooking on the stove. Katie, the miracle-woman in my life, the woman who can write books and operate an electric drill and grow prize-winning flowers, will be bringing another masterpiece soup to completion.

I'll taste it and savor it and give thanks that in this room, in this moment, all my wishes have come true.

CHAPTER SIX

FOR YOU

How to Ignite
Your Power Within

And now the precious moment arrives.

I turn to you and invite you to take the journey for yourself.

In the years since my conversation with Ed, I've had thousands of conversations in which I asked clients, friends, and family to tell me their wishes. Based on this experience I've expanded and refined the process in many ways. In this chapter I want to take you through the Five Wishes process exactly as I would if you were sitting in my office with me. As we go along, I'll also give you examples and stories of how others have used the process.

I've created a Five Wishes worksheet to facilitate the process. If you'd like to print out one to write on, you can do so at www.5wishesbook.com. Otherwise, you can write in a notebook or journal, or in this book.

When I work with people on their Five Wishes, I begin with a brief explanation followed by an invitation. Picture me saying to you, "In my thirties I received the gift of a question that changed the course of my life. My decision to answer that question gave me a life in which all my dreams came true. Now I want to offer you that gift, so you can use its gentle power to create your own fulfilled life."

Then I make the invitation to you. I ask, "Are you willing to receive the gift of the question, and use it to create your own fulfilled life?"

If you say, "Yes," I ask you to imagine yourself on your deathbed, now or fifty years from now.

I come to visit you. I stand by your bed and ask, "Was your life a complete success?"

You say, "Yes," or you say, "No."

If you say, "No," what are the reasons that your life hasn't been a complete success? Take time to write them down. Don't let yourself wriggle out of doing it right now. Remember what Ed said: "The bigger the question, the more important it is to answer it right now. This moment is all the time you need. It's the only one we have."

Go ahead. Take out a piece of paper (or use the worksheet), and do it now. Just write out the sentence below and fill in the blank with what's true for you. Begin with the most important one. First, phrase it in a negative way; as Ed said, doing this "has a marvelous way of clearing the mind."

✦

The main reason my life was not a total success is because I didn't

_____.

Now write down your remaining four reasons.

My life was not a complete success because I didn't

_____.

My life was not a complete success because I didn't

_____.

My life was not a complete success because I didn't

_____.

My life was not a complete success because I didn't

_____.

✦

Then reread the first one to make sure it's the most important; if it's not, revise the order. When you're sure, turn these statements into your wishes:

✦

For my life to have been a total success I wish I'd

_____.

And I wish I'd

_____.

I also wish I'd

_____.

And

_____.

And

_____.

*If I'd done or experienced these things,
I'd consider my life a success.*

✦

EMOTIONS AND LIMITING BELIEFS

As you do the Five Wishes process, you're likely to stir up emotions and encounter limiting beliefs. If that happens for you, it's a good thing. It means the process is working. One of the purposes of the process is to bring your feelings and limiting beliefs into the light so you can be aware of them and release them. It's important to welcome all your emotions and limiting beliefs as you move through the process.

The emotions that get triggered most often are sadness, anger, and fear. Sometimes you'll get all three at once. Regardless of what comes up, though, just open the door and say, "Welcome."

The same is true for limiting beliefs. As you work with the Five Wishes process you'll come face-to-face with old programs that got installed earlier in your life, often without your even knowing it. In fact, I've found that more often than not, most of us don't realize a limiting belief is just a limiting belief. We take it as reality — the way things have to be. I've seen dozens of people experience the happy surprise of realizing that a limitation they'd taken as real and permanent was just an imaginary corral they were keeping themselves penned inside of.

Some of the most common limiting beliefs are:

I'm too old to _____.

I don't have enough money to _____.

I'm not smart enough to _____.

I have to wait until _____

before I can _____.

Let me give you a good example. I did a Five Wishes session with Dora, a woman in her fifties. She and her husband had divorced after a marriage she described as "long, dull, and distant." When the children had grown up, she and her husband had drifted even further apart and then had gone their separate ways. On the worksheet she wrote, "The main reason my life was not a success was because I never knew what real happiness was." The moment she finished writing it down she burst into tears. I invited her to be with her sadness, to welcome it and accept it.

I've often noticed that people tend to hold their breath when their emotions come up. I remember doing that myself when I was a kid, to try to keep myself from crying. When I saw Dora holding her breath and crying at the same time, I invited her to use her breathing to welcome her sadness instead of trying to shut it out by holding her breath. I showed her how to take easy, deep breaths while feeling the sensations of the sadness, such as the lump in her throat and the burning sensation of the tears. She suddenly said she felt cold. I knew from past experience that people often feel cold when they're scared, so I asked her to scan her body for fear sensations such as the speedy, slightly queasy feeling in the stomach that many people call "butterflies." She nodded and said she felt scared. I invited her to listen to her fear and find out what it was about. "I'm afraid I'll never be happy," she said.

As I mentioned earlier, people often don't realize that a belief is just a belief. When I asked Dora where she picked up the belief that she couldn't be happy, she blinked in astonishment. "That's not exactly what I'd call a belief. Who do you ever see walking around looking like they're happy?" Somehow she had generalized her limiting belief to include all humanity. I asked her, though, to think back through time to when she might have first encountered the idea that people couldn't be happy. I saw a look of irritation and disgust flicker across her face. I asked what she'd just thought of.

"My grandmother," she said. "The bitterest human being I've ever met."

She then told me a three-generation story of betrayal and heartbreak, in which both her grandmother and her mother had been left alone and ultimately destitute by the death or departure of several different husbands. An insight came to her:

"I wonder if that's why I picked my husband," she said. "I knew from when I first met him that he wasn't right for me, but I also knew he would never leave me or betray me." This awareness brought another flood of tears. "That's not a very high goal to set for a marriage, is it? To just have somebody not leave you." I told her it was understandable, given her background, but that the important thing was to realize that she didn't need to be confined within that or any other limiting belief any longer.

There's a great value in welcoming your emotions and your limiting beliefs into the light: once they're revealed to you, they lose their grip. As Dora and I did as we went through the process, think about what has been holding you back from achieving your Five Wishes thus far. What experiences or tendencies in your past have led to your limiting beliefs? Now is the time to uncover and deprogram them.

With Dora, I noticed a new lightness in her face and her tone of voice as we continued through the process.

These are the Five Wishes she came up with:

✦

For my life to have been a success, I wish I'd been genuinely happy.

And I wish I'd spent more time doing things for my own development.

I also wish I'd known what it felt like to be in love.

And found some cause or passion bigger than myself to dedicate my life to.

And had a job I really enjoyed.

✦

COMMITTING TO LIFE

Contrast Dora's first wish with that of Connie, a thirty-year-old woman:

✦

For my life to have been a success, I wish I'd played passionately all the way through.

✦

As Connie and I worked with this wish, the emotion that came up was a fear of getting trapped in a stagnant job and a marriage that limited her freedom. She had felt the joy of full, passionate commitment through her work with an environmental organization. Also, she was in a close relationship with a man whom she'd been with for several years. The relationship gave her room to take off by herself on solo travels and seminars without having to explain or justify. But now she was feeling pressure from her family to settle down, get a "real job," and marry her man. Her family provided some of the funding for her adventures, so she was inclined to heed their opinions, perhaps more than the average thirty-year-old would be.

Underlying her wish for passionate engagement with life is the fear that she may settle for a life of restraints and routine. Here is why I invited you to contrast Dora's experience with Connie's: both of them, in their own way, are grappling with one of life's most crucial issues, the choice to play the game of life with full-on commitment or to watch from the bench, to root, grumble, or doze until the whistle blows. Connie stands on the sidelines, trying to avoid being benched forever, while Dora looks back in despair that she benched herself a long time ago. She's suffering the consequences of a long-ago choice that most of us don't even realize is a choice. (I sure didn't realize it was a choice until after I had sunk into a deep trance of mediocrity in my twenties. Like the James Joyce character, Mr. Duffy, I was living "a short distance from my body," an absentee-landlord of my own life.)

One of the beautiful things about the Five Wishes process is that you can do it at any time in your life, regardless of your age or life circumstance. It's never too late to figure out what's essential. Dora produced genuine magic in her life, and it didn't take much time to do it. As we moved into the final stage of the process, she turned her wishes into right-now, present-tense goals. Her wish for genuine happiness became, "I feel happy wherever I go and whatever I'm doing." I invited her to speak that sentence out loud a number of times until she felt at home with this idea, which an hour before would have seemed unthinkable, even outrageous. As she pronounced the sentence over and over, a smile appeared at the corners of her mouth. I asked what she was feeling.

She said she was nervous and excited, but "there's something else, too."

I asked her to describe it. She said it was like a welcoming space around the outside of her nervousness and excitement. Now I got excited, because I've always believed that happiness is more than a feeling — it's a feeling about all your feelings. It's a subtle, pleasant sensation that comes from being open to your emotions, open to the present moment, open to life. Dora was describing it exactly that way.

"Congratulations," I said. "You're already making good on your biggest goal, feeling happy wherever you are and whatever you're doing." Her smile got bigger.

"Now it's just a matter of practice," I said.

As for Connie, after working with her Five Wishes, she decided to resist the pressures of her family and not settle for less in order to please them. She thanked them for their support in the past, but chose to accept no more financial gifts from them. After several short-term consulting jobs, she found work she enjoyed: organizing and leading eco-travel journeys.

YOUR FIVE WISHES
IN THE HERE AND NOW

It's time to turn your wishes into goals. Put them in the present tense, as if they were happening now. Begin with the most important one. For example, let's say you wrote:

The main reason my life was not a total success is because I never found my soul mate.

Here's one way you might word this as a positive, present-tense statement:

My life is a total success because I'm now thriving in a loving relationship with my soul mate.

Now it's your turn. Write out your most important goal like this:

✦

My life is a total success because I'm now

_____

_____.

✦

Read it over a few times. Say it out loud. Find out if it's something that resonates in your heart and soul.

Assuming it does, let's move on to your other wishes and goals. As you did with your first wish, turn the other four wishes into goals. Word them in the present tense as if they were happening now.

✦

My life is a complete success because I'm now

_____.

It's also a success because I'm now

_____.

And I'm now

_____.

And I'm now

_____.

And I'm now

_____.

ACTION STEPS

One thing you'll probably find helpful is to create action steps that will translate your goals into practical reality. Sometimes the action steps are quite obvious; other times you have to get creative to come up with your next step. Here is an example of what I mean, from one of my friends, Sandy.

Sandy came by one afternoon while I was working on this book. She and Kathlyn came back into my study to bring me a cup of tea, and after hearing what I was up to, Sandy wanted to experience the Five Wishes process. Fifteen minutes later she had generated this list:

✦

*For my life to have been a complete success I wish
I'd found work and a career I really loved.*

*And I wish I'd seen the pyramids and the Taj
Mahal in person.*

And also I wish I'd finished my master's degree.

*And kept writing poetry after my
two boys were born.*

*And spent more time with my
husband just doing fun things.*

✦

Here are Sandy's wishes turned into present-
tense goals.

✦

*My life is a total success because
I'm now enjoying work and a career I love.*

*I'm also a success because I have toured the
pyramids and the Taj Mahal.*

*And I'm enjoying the completion
of my master's degree.*

And I'm now writing poetry every day.

And I'm spending lots of fun time with Paul.

✦

Her list illustrates something you'll probably find as you do your own Five Wishes: some items are things you can do right now, while others will take some time to put into place. For example, Sandy still had a year to go on her master's degree, so even if the university would let her resume her studies (it had been ten years, so there was some question about whether she could pick up where she left off), she would still have quite a bit of work to do before that wish could become a reality. Her fourth wish, though, was something she could do right away. In fact, I chose this one to focus on first in helping her generate an action step.

I asked her what she could do as a first step in starting to write poetry again. She listed off a number of things, such as getting the kind of notebook she liked, creating time to write, and so on. I challenged her on this idea; it seemed like a limiting belief to think she had to have a certain kind of notebook, uninterrupted time, or anything more than what she had right that moment. I handed her a blank piece of paper and a pen. "See? You could write a poem right now." She laughed out loud. "I get it," she said. "I can write a poem anytime." Over the next half hour, Sandy wrote several, and although she judged them as less than stellar, at least she was a practicing poet again.

Sandy got an immediate surge of energy and clarity from writing down her deathbed wishes and goals. "It snapped my life into focus," she told me a few months afterward. "I felt a sense of renewed purpose about what my life was all about."

The experience also produced some immediate real-world results in her life. "I kept writing, and soon I wrote the first good poem I'd written in ages," she told me. "That poem opened the floodgates to about twenty more poems I've written since then. I told my husband about all this, and told him that one of my goals was to spend more quality time with him. That brought a smile to his face, and we made an agreement on the spot to build a date-night into our schedule every week."

Some of her other goals — developing a career she loves, completing her master's degree, and seeing the Taj Mahal — will take time to complete, but she's made a list of action steps for each one, so she's on her way. In the meantime, she is surfing a fresh wave of energy and creative exhilaration from the process. In time she will visit the Taj Mahal and the pyramids. She may also explore the mysteries of other places as yet undreamed of. Goals are never carved in stone; they can always be revisited and revised in light of new discoveries about yourself.

Take a look at your goals. Are there action steps that you can begin taking right away to make them happen? Spend time brainstorming those steps, and write them down. Seek out resources to help you to attain your specific goals — books, classes, like-minded people, and so on. Keep up the momentum of your Five Wishes process by following through with your action steps and tracking your progress.

BACK TALK

Throughout the process, be aware of what I call *back talk*: the mind chatter and other reactions that happen when you introduce a more positive idea into your system. Your mind's beliefs are based on your old programming, so naturally your mind will rebel when you introduce a brilliant, positive new idea to it. Back talk is like the reactions of the established authorities when a new idea is introduced. When Copernicus and Galileo started introducing their new ideas, for example, the authorities got pretty stirred up. *Wait a minute*, the authorities said, *it's obvious that the sun goes around the earth! Hold on*, the authorities said, *it's obvious that the earth is flat!* Our minds work in just the same way, so expect some back talk when you introduce the radical idea that you can fulfill your deepest wishes.

When you state a positive new idea in your head or out loud, you'll probably notice back talk right away. It may come from your mind, your body, your emotions, or all three at once. I want you to be aware of back talk, and even to welcome it.

Welcome the back talk, because it's completely natural and normal. It's actually a sign that the new idea you've planted in your mind is taking root. For example, let's say your wish is "My life is a total success because I'm now thriving in a loving relationship with my soul mate." The moment you say it to yourself or out loud, your mind might fire off a stream of back talk, such as "That's impossible!" or "Forget it, pal, nobody in your family has ever had one of those." Back talk might show up in your body and your emotions, maybe as a wave of sadness, a twinge of tension, or a clenched jaw. Accept any and all back talk — it's a quick way to learn what your barriers have been to realizing the goal. For example, if your back talk comes in the form of a wave of sadness, it's likely that some old undigested sadness has been standing in the way of you finding a partner and developing a loving relationship. That's good to know — it will help you grow compassion for yourself.

The best attitude to take toward back talk is to reach out and embrace it with love, compassion, and understanding. No need to criticize it for its shortcomings or to waste time in recriminations. Just give a loving nod and a hug to any back talk you get, and move on to the joyful creation of your fulfilled life.

TAILORING YOUR FIVE WISHES

After you come up with five wishes that feel good and right to you, stay open to further modifications of them as you move through your life. Think of your five wishes as a wonderful new wardrobe of clothes you're wearing. Glance in a mirror now and then to see how they fit. Make little adjustments so they'll fit better, by improving the wording of them or replacing them with new wishes that feel better. However, before replacing a wish, ask yourself, *Am I abandoning it simply because I think it's too hard to accomplish?* A good way to answer this question is with another question: *If it were not hard to accomplish, would I still want it?* Let me give you an example. Jerry is now deceased, but even though it's been more than three decades since I first met him, he still inspires me with his courage and dedication. In his mid-forties he had a life crisis in which he realized he hated being a lawyer. He realized he'd always wanted to be a physician but had gone into law because of family pressures and because he didn't think he was smart enough for medical school. In mid-life, he could not find a medical school in the United States that would take him. Stymied, he faced the despair of going through the rest of his life with a major unfulfilled dream. Fortunately, he asked himself the question, *If it were not hard to accomplish, would I still want it?* He got a resounding *Yes*, so he kept his wish to attend medical school at the very top of his list. Suddenly a new possibility opened up. He found a medical school in Holland that would take him. In fact, they had an opening in six weeks! One little problem: all the lectures were in Dutch. It seemed impossibly hard to learn enough Dutch in six weeks to comprehend medical lectures, but again, he asked himself, *If it were not hard to accomplish, would I still want it? Of course!* Over the next six weeks he studied and spoke Dutch eighteen hours a day, and when he sat down for his first class he even took notes in Dutch. After years of schooling, internship, and residency, he began practice in his fifties. The last time I saw him, he was still a vibrant and engaged member of the medical profession as he neared eighty.

WHAT MATTERS MOST

In my experience, both in my own life and in working with people for the past thirty-some years, I've found that we human beings have a great deal more capacity for achieving our goals than we usually give ourselves credit for. I believe we can attain all the important goals of our lifetimes — if we get our hearts and minds into harmony about what those goals are. I had five goals that were important to me. You may have more or less than that; the number does not matter. Ultimately, the only thing that matters is the quality of your goals and how they resonate within you.

From the perspective of your deathbed, what matters is that your final breath comes in with the sweet satisfaction of a life fulfilled and goes out with the blessing of a life complete. From the perspective of right now, what matters is that your next breath energizes your intention to fulfill your destiny.

I'll always be grateful that a stranger at a party asked me a question that challenged me to change my life. I'm also very grateful that I get to present these possibilities and choices to you. Writing this book continues to bring my third wish toward fulfillment.

Now, our journey together, at least in this form, draws to a close. I want to thank you for opening your heart and mind to the living miracles we've explored together in this book. Please carry my heartfelt blessing with you:

✦

Wherever your path takes you, may all your deathbed wishes come true, and may you celebrate each and every one of them many long years before your final breath.

✦

RESOURCES

The Five Wishes
Website and Movie

THE FIVE WISHES WEBSITE:
WWW.5WISHESBOOK.COM

You'll find a wealth of resources at www.5wishes book.com. I want to call your attention to several of them that I think you'll find particularly useful.

First, we're growing a thriving Five Wishes community at the website, and I'd like you to be part of it so you can benefit from the synergies of others who are moving along the same path as you. At the website you'll discover several ways of forming Five Wishes groups, either virtually, over the phone, or in person. I also host free teleconference classes on different aspects of the Five Wishes material; check the website for the schedule.

Second, you'll find a specially developed system for posting your five wishes so that others can read them. You can post either anonymously or with your real name, as you prefer. There's also a section of the website for posting your completions, the process I describe in the chapter on my second wish. I think you'll be amazed by the energy boost you'll get from posting your wishes and completions, and from reading the posts of others.

Third, we're always updating the Five Wishes worksheet and providing new materials, so be sure to visit the website periodically to see the latest versions of all the free materials. You'll also find audio and video clips of people working on their five wishes.

FIVE WISHES: THE MOVIE

I've been a movie lover as long as I can remember; even as a kid I had a feeling I'd be involved with movies someday. As you may know, Kathlyn and I, along with Stephen Simon, cofounded the Spiritual

Cinema Circle and in 2004 began to distribute what we call "movies that matter." At the time of this writing, we have members in more than eighty countries around the world who get our monthly compilation of shorts, features, and documentaries. We also produced an original feature, *Conversations with God*, as well as other, shorter films.

After I finished writing the first draft of this book, which I'd worked on night and day for many months, I wanted to let my mind rest up from the intensity of the writing process. My intention was to set aside the book and not even think about it for a week or so. My mind, however, seemed to have a different idea. One night I woke up just past 3 AM in the hot grip of something brand-new and totally unexpected: I wanted to write and make a short film based on the first part of the book, the conversation with Ed that started it all.

This project got such a grip on me that within a month I had written the script, green-lighted its production, and assembled a terrific cast. Kathlyn was essential in making it happen; in her role as executive producer she handled all the details, arranged the casting sessions, manifested the funds to make the movie, and graciously played host to dozens of people involved in the process.

I knew from the beginning the lead actor and director I wanted: Michael Goorjian. I had admired his work as an actor in many movies, particularly *Hard Rain* with Morgan Freeman. I had also been deeply impressed by his skills as a director in the Kirk Douglas film *Illusion*, in which he also starred alongside Douglas. In addition, he happened to be exactly the same age that I was when the conversation with Ed took place. I asked Michael to play me and to direct the movie; to my great delight, he agreed. After looking at lots of actors to play Ed, Michael suggested that I play the role myself. At first I gulped at this suggestion. I'd been on hundreds of television and radio talk shows, but I'd never acted in a movie or a play. Eventually I got over my nervousness enough to see the wisdom of the idea. Not only had I been present for the original conversation with Ed; I was now the same age that Ed was when he asked me the big question that changed my life.

I'm very proud of the movie, which turned out even better than I dared hope. It comes in at just under twenty minutes and tells the story of the party, the conversation, and the realizations that flowed from it. Part of the magic came from the cast and crew becoming enthralled with the Five Wishes process as well as the story. It was deeply satisfying to see them poring over their worksheets during lunch breaks and discussing their five wishes with each other. The movie became a transformational experience for all of us, and I hope it will be the same for you. As an example of how the cast and crew engaged with their five wishes, I'd like to share with you part of the Five Wishes process I did with Michael, the director and lead actor.

Michael is not only a gifted actor and director; he also has a passionate interest in exploring the psychological and spiritual depths in himself and others. He contrasts sharply with a great many actors I've met, even some very famous ones, who have about as much personal depth as a blueberry pancake. When I suggested to Michael that I take him through the same process Ed took me through when I was thirty-four, he immediately said yes.

Our conversation went like this:

"Ready?" I asked. He said he was.

"Michael, imagine you're on your deathbed, today or fifty years from now, and I come by to visit. I ask you, 'Was your life a complete success?'"

He closed his eyes, getting the picture.

"Would you say 'Yes' or 'No'?"

After a moment's pause he answered. "I'd have to say 'No.'"

"Why is that?"

"I wouldn't say it was a complete failure, but it wasn't a success because I didn't live up to the potential I felt I had."

I asked, "What's the main area in which you haven't lived up to your potential?"

"The main one is that I haven't developed myself on an inner level yet to the point where I know why I'm alive. I really want to know why I'm here. I haven't quite formed my own sense of being yet. Some people accept a faith — that gives them a sense of being. Some people just don't care

— they put their attention on something else. I'm not either one of those kinds of people. I really want to know why I'm here."

I asked him if there were other reasons his life was not a success.

He said, "I don't feel like I've created what I think I can create. I've done some good work, but I don't think I've done a truly masterful performance or created a masterful work of art."

We took a moment to resonate with those powerful statements. I was moved by his ability to articulate them so beautifully and simply. He went further, saying, "The generation I grew up in had such a cynicism about asking those kinds of questions. We were the children of the Me-Generation parents who meditated and went to Esalen and made us go to therapy with them. So naturally, we rebelled against anything that smacked of spirituality or self-inquiry. I'm over being embarrassed by all that. Now I just want to know."

I summarized what he'd said into two wishes. "You wish you'd discovered who you really are and your purpose for being here. That's number one."

He nodded.

"Second, you wish you had expressed yourself fully in the creative realm."

He added, "Yes. I also want acknowledgment and fame and other ego stuff that's mixed in there."

I asked him to identify a work he could create that would tie the two wishes together.

"I wish I'd created a film that expressed the ideas I felt were important, a piece of art that's about who we really are and why we're here."

I asked him to put those wishes into the present tense, so that he would have affirmations to guide him.

He phrased the first wish this way:

"I have a deep understanding of why I'm alive on this earth."

And his second wish this way:

"I make art that fully expresses the ideas that I cherish."

I invited him to hold both of those ideas in

the loving arms of an intention to thrive in every way. He responded with:

"My work is received so well that I always have plenty of money to live a magnificent life and create more great works of art."

I invited him to say these sentences over and over until he felt a harmonious resonance with them in his body and mind. I watched his face carefully while he repeated the wishes over and over for a minute or so. Suddenly I saw the sign I was looking for: a smile broke out on his face as he experienced the "Aaaahhhh" of connection, the moment when the new ideas in his mind touched the place in his body that resonated with their truth and possibility.

I'm happy to report that since Michael did his Five Wishes, he's had a steady stream of acting and directing jobs, including a major role created specially for him in the spin-off of the popular TV series *24*. I look forward to what the future will bring for this gifted young man.

ACKNOWLEDGMENTS

First, I would like to thank Neale Donald Walsch for inspiring me to write this book. His insight, guidance, and loving presence are precious to me. Thank you, Neale, for your gifts to the world.

Thinking of Ed Steinbrecher always brings a smile to my face and a warm feeling of gratitude to my heart. Although we only saw each other fleetingly during his time on earth, he has been and will always be an anchor point for me.

I appreciate the loving attention given to this book by Marc Allen and his colleagues at New World Library. Kristen Cashman's insightful and delicate editorial touch was especially helpful.

Bonnie Solow is not only a great literary agent but also a dear friend and trusted advisor. Kathlyn and I both adore her and are deeply grateful for her presence in our lives.

I owe a deep bow of gratitude to the thousands of people with whom I've had Five Wishes conversations over the years. You helped me understand and deepen the process in myriad ways. I only hope you've benefited as much as I have from the conversations.

I'm blessed to be surrounded by a loving family and a wonderful circle of friends, nearby and far-flung, who give my life a glow I feel in every moment. To Amanda, Chris, Helen, Mike, Elsie, Imogen, and the other members of our quirky clan, eternal thanks for the love you've given me and the examples you're setting through your creative, contributive lives. To Monika Krajewska, Stephen Simon, Arielle Ford, and other members of our team, thank you for showing me that work and love are indistinguishable.

To Kathlyn, my wife and creative collaborator, my gratitude is boundless. I've had the rare pleasure of waking up every day for twenty-seven years now feeling like the luckiest man on earth, and if genes, gods, and good living favor us with another twenty-seven (or more), I'll still be counting my lucky stars.

ABOUT THE AUTHOR

GAY HENDRICKS is an internationally famous author, seminar leader, web entrepreneur, and filmmaker. He received his PhD in counseling psychology from Stanford University in 1974 and is the author of more than twenty books, including the national bestsellers *Conscious Loving, Conscious Living,* and *The Corporate Mystic.* He is the founder of several organizations, including the Hendricks Institute, the Foundation for Conscious Living, the Spiritual Cinema Circle, and Illumination University. He also lectures widely and has a weekly radio show on Hay House Radio. He resides with his wife, author and seminar leader Kathlyn Hendricks, in Ojai, California. For more information, see www.hendricks.com.

Our products are available
in bookstores everywhere.
For our catalog, please contact:

New World Library
14 Pamaron Way
Novato, California 94949

Phone: 415-884-2100 or 800-972-6657
Catalog requests: Ext. 50
Orders: Ext. 52
Fax: 415-884-2199
Email: escort@newworldlibrary.com

To subscribe to our electronic newsletter, visit
www.newworldlibrary.com